10 MINUTE GUIDE TO

BEATING DEBT

D1056261

by Susan Abentrod

alpha
books

ARCO

Macmillan Spectrum/Alpha

A Division of Macmillan General Reference
A Simon & Schuster Macmillan Company
1633 Broadway, New York, NY 10019-6785

International Standard Book Number: 0-02-861115-2
Library of Congress Catalog Card Number: 96-68550

98 97 96   8 7 6 5 4 3 2 1

Interpretation of the printing code: the rightmost double-digit number is the year of the book's first printing; the rightmost single-digit number is the number of the book's printing. For example, a printing code of 96-1 shows that this copy of the book was printed during the first printing of the book in 1996.

Printed in the United States of America

Publisher Theresa Murtha

Managing Editors Brian Phair and Michael E. Cunningham

Development Editor Debra Wishik Englander

Production Editor Maureen A. Schneeberger

Cover Designer Dan Armstrong

Designer Kim Scott

Indexer Chris Wilcox

Production Team Heather Butler, Angela Calvert, Daniel Caparo, Terrie Deemer, Scott Tullis, Christine Tyner, Christy Wagner

CONTENTS

INTRODUCTION

Money is freedom. It gives you power. It gives you choices. Life is less scary when you have it. And it's fun to spend, even when the money you're spending isn't really yours.

That's the problem. It's easy to get into the habit of spending money before you earn it. Every day, you're tempted to treat yourself by buying items that only a few people can afford to purchase on a regular basis.

It's all too easy to lose sight of how to spend your money, especially if you only have a vague idea of what it takes to make ends meet.

This book is about gaining control of your money, and money is about control. You will learn to stop and think before you buy. Find money to invest. Get out from under debt. Keep your credit spending in line. In short, you must take control of your money, or it will take control of you.

There is one major objective to this book—to make the process of successful money management as painless as possible.

When you're in control of your money, you will still be able to reward yourself. When you learn to budget, you'll realize that you can strike a balance between being financially responsible and still doing the things you love. You'll look at ways to save money in areas you never thought about.

This book is written so that it progresses from the first critical steps of organization and goal setting to lessons on getting out of debt and avoiding problems in the future. If you're sure you are in trouble now and need immediate help, then go right to Lesson 14.

The *10 Minute Guide to Beating Debt* will guide you through the steps you need to take in order to get out of trouble now and avoid debt problems in the future. Each 10 minute lesson will present you with concepts and ideas that you can do quickly to get on the right path to financial security.

CONVENTIONS USED IN THIS BOOK

The *10 Minute Guide to Beating Debt* uses the following icons to identify helpful information:

Timesaver Tip icons help you save time when carrying out suggestions in this book.

Plain English icons appear to define new terms.

Panic Button icons identify problems and how to solve them.

UNDERSTANDING DEBT

In this lesson, you'll learn the characteristics of debt and how borrowing money can affect your financial security.

Making big purchases, going on vacation, and meeting day-to-day expenses take large amounts of both money and planning. When you want to buy something but don't have the money available to pay for it outright, you only have a few choices.

You could decide to wait, and save the money before you spend it. But saving money takes time—and emergencies don't wait. So, you must borrow, and with borrowing comes debt, which means you owe money to someone else.

LEARNING ABOUT DEBT

When you need money, and don't have it yourself, you borrow. Generally you borrow from a bank. Banks and other financial institutions lend money in order to make money by charging you what is known as interest on the amount you borrow, known as the principal.

Principal   The amount of money you borrow.

Your ability to make purchases immediately by borrowing has a cost. You pay interest for the privilege of using someone else's money. The rate you pay will vary from lender to lender.

 Interest   The fee you're charged for borrowing money from others.

When you make purchases using a charge or credit card, you're backing your purchase with your honor to pay back the amount in full.

 Credit   An amount of money made available for your control by a bank or other lender.

Buying on credit can make life easier by allowing you to take possession of goods before you've saved up the money to pay for them.

 Credit Cards   Credit cards allow you to borrow up to a set limit. You can pay them back at your own pace, but you must pay a minimum amount each month along with interest.

Charge Cards   Charge cards are similar to credit cards, except they are issued by retailers. They also have a monthly minimum and charge interest on unpaid balances.

Two of the biggest problems with using credit are charging more than you should and not paying it back on time. See Lesson 16 on how to avoid getting in over your head.

 Credit Control   Before you charge any items, ask yourself, "How are you going to pay the money back? Is the item you're buying essential to your well being?"

RIGHT AND WRONG REASONS FOR USING DEBT

When making large purchases like a house, a car, or paying for a college education, the cost is often so substantial that it may be impossible for you to save the money up in advance. That's when borrowing money and carrying debt makes the most sense.

In Lesson 8, there's more information on good sense borrowing.

There are also other good reasons for carrying debt. Here's a list to help you determine the right reasons for using debt in your financial planning:

- To buy a home
- To make permanent improvements on your home
- To start a business
- To go to school
- To buy a car
- To invest (nothing is guaranteed, but in stable long-term investments such as blue chip stocks, growth has been nine to ten percent yearly over the past 70 years)
- For money you need only for a short while

Here are the reasons you should avoid borrowing money:

- To bail someone else out of financial problems
- To go on vacation
- To give to the kids to start a business
- To invest in a stock tip
- To buy clothes
- To lend to your friends
- To gamble
- To get married
- To donate to a political campaign

The problem with debt occurs not when you borrow, but when you fail to pay off the loan according to the agreed upon terms. If you don't use debt wisely by paying it off on time, you can destroy your credit rating and have problems borrowing money later.

LOOKING AT TYPES OF DEBT

There are basically two types of debt, secured and unsecured. Secured debt is backed by your possessions. Unsecured debt is backed by your word.

 Secured debt   Loans backed by property or assets that you own.

Both car loans and mortgages are secured loans. If, for some reason, you're not able to pay these loans back, you'll have your car repossessed or lose your house through foreclosure. Either way, you lose the money that you've paid as well as the items you borrowed for in the first place.

Some banks will let you back your loans with savings accounts or investments, known as collateral. Often, you are able to borrow a portion of their value as a kind of insurance policy that the bank will eventually get their money back.

 Unsecured debt   These loans don't require any assets to back up your word to repay. Instead, you give your word (full faith and credit) that you will pay back the loan.

With unsecured loans such as credit cards, creditors lend you money based on whether you're deemed creditworthy. When you take out these loans, you're making a promise that the total amount will be paid, based on some predetermined schedule.

Failing to Repay If you fall behind in payments or fail to make good on your word, your credit rating will suffer and you can probably expect legal action to be taken against you.

 Co-signer If you have trouble getting a loan on your own, get someone to add his or her guarantee to the note. He or she guarantees that the loan will be paid back according to the terms of the note.

Remember, it's your responsibility to pay back your own loans. If you have someone co-sign for you, legal action can be taken against them if you fail to repay.

In this lesson, you've learned the typical kinds of debt available to you and some of the right and wrong reasons to borrow. In the next lesson, you will learn to evaluate your financial situation.

EVALUATING YOUR SITUATION

*In this lesson, you'll learn how to determine if you owe
more than you should and what some of the most
common explanations are for having more debt than you
can handle.*

DO YOU HAVE A PROBLEM?

If you owe more than you should, you may already know it. If
you have trouble meeting your monthly bills and have creditors calling for payment, these are two sure signs that you owe
too much.

Lenders don't always have all the information to determine
whether you're overextended. They don't know what your job
is or whether you're in the midst of having a personal crisis.

With credit card issuers charging upwards of 18 percent interest, these credit card companies obviously increase their prof-
its every time you charge more than you can pay back at the
end of the month.

Rule of Thumb Lenders usually believe you can spend 28 percent of total income on home expenses (mortgage, taxes, insurance). Total borrowing (mortgage + auto + credit card debt) shouldn't exceed 36 percent.

 Loan Limits Lenders base your borrowing limits on many things like earning power, past credit history, debts, and even unused credit card limits.

You have to balance what creditors will lend you with what you can comfortably repay.

If any of the following scenarios are familiar to you, then you're probably headed for trouble in the future:

You find...

> You never have enough money set aside for a rainy day
>
> You have to borrow to meet day-to-day expenses
>
> Your creditors call and write you for payment
>
> You constantly fight with your loved ones over money
>
> You gamble—and lose

ACCEPTING RESPONSIBILITY

If debt even one of these signs of trouble applies to you, you should take responsibility to get things back in order now.

Regardless of the reasons you got in trouble in the first place, the problems won't be solved until you're willing to take responsibility for your actions and work on repaying your debt.

It's so much easier when you can blame someone else. However, if you're having financial problems, admitting that you're the one responsible for them is the first crucial step to correcting the problem. After all, you're the one who must learn to stop using your credit cards and borrowing money.

Often, understanding why you got into trouble in the first place can help you change your spending habits.

TRACKING CAUSES OF DEBT

Write down a list of the things you do that lead to financial distress.

Concentrate Ask your spouse to help you. He or she may recognize spending habits that you're not aware you have.

This is the time for some serious self-evaluation. When you've completed the list, study it. While you can create the list together, only you can work to overcome the symptoms you see in front of you.

Here's another exercise that should help. Take out your monthly loan and credit card statements and find the outstanding balance. Write the balance down on the worksheet shown in figure 2.1.

LENDER	AMOUNT	REASON

Figure 2.1 Reasons for borrowing.

Now, try to recall when you made the purchase. What led to the debt in the first place? Think of all the possible reasons and list them on the chart.

Once you get a handle on what got you into trouble, you can work to avoid it in the future and begin to take steps to get yourself on track.

In this lesson, you learned how to tell if you have too much debt. You should now be more familiar with some of the common problems associated with accumulating debt. In the next lesson, you will learn how to set goals.

GOAL SETTING

In this lesson, you'll learn how to organize your goals and list them in order of priority so you can start to gain control of your finances.

In order for you to be in control of your finances, it's important for you to decide what you want to accomplish.

Setting up goals is important for everyone's fiscal fitness, but it's critical when you're trying to get out of debt.

Goal Something you want to accomplish—a target, a dream.

Objective Specific things you want to achieve within a certain time frame.

Priority Placing items in order of importance.

DEVELOPING YOUR LIST

One of the first steps to financial management is to decide what you want to do with your money. You need specific target goals.

Having a list of goals will help you get out of debt in two ways:

- You'll begin to focus on strategies that will allow you to pay off current debt.

- You'll be able to set up strategies to help you get the things you want without having to go deep into debt in the future.

Paying Off Debt   If you have extra cash in the bank, it usually makes sense to pay off outstanding debts if the interest you're earning on the money is less than the interest you're repaying. For example, if you have $5,000 in a savings account which earns $250 a year (at five percent interest) and you are paying $900 in interest on your debt, you should pay off the balance on your card instead of leaving your money in the bank.

Remember, financial planning works only if you have specific goals to work toward. The most important item in the financial picture is you—what do you want and when do you want it.

In this lesson, you learned ways to uncover your financial goals and begin focusing on them in order of importance. In Lesson 4, you'll start to get organized.

GETTING ORGANIZED

In this lesson, you'll learn how to get and keep your financial records in order. You will also learn how long you should keep your financial papers and where they should be kept.

Here are four reasons to get organized:

- You'll know what you have
- You'll know what needs to be updated
- You'll save time looking for things
- You can simplify your life

HOW LONG TO KEEP MOST RECORDS

Sort everything into two piles: things you need to keep and things you can throw away. How do you know which is which? Use the following guidelines to help.

Things to keep for one year:

- Cancelled checks for non-tax-deductible items only
- Receipts for food and clothing

- Utility bills

- Insurance policies (with no outstanding claims)

 Budget Tip   Before you throw out any receipts, use them to help you set up a monthly budget (see Lesson 5).

Papers to keep for seven years:

- All income-tax records

- All supporting documentation for tax records

- Cancelled checks for deductible expenses

Papers to keep for as long as you own the item:

- Mortgage papers

- Home improvement records

- Titles to cars and boats

- Receipts on items requiring insurance

- Contracts

Papers to keep forever:

- Birth certificates

- Marriage licenses

- Wills and trusts

- Military papers

- Divorce papers

These lists should help. It's easiest to start with the things you can throw away after one year. Once you've completed that category, you can go on from there.

What about the things you need to keep? Start with the paper-
work that would be most difficult to replace such as your birth
certificate or deed to your house. These should be stored in
either a safe-deposit box at the bank (which will cost about
$20 per year) or in a fireproof safe in your home (which will
cost between $40 and $55).

Household Inventory   Go through your home
and make an inventory of your possessions. Make
a list of every item or use a camera to take photos.
Either way, these records will be invaluable if you
have to file an insurance claim if these items are
lost or stolen.

FILING YOUR RECORDS

The rest of your papers can be organized into files and put in a
filing cabinet.

Flag   To help keep you on top of outdated
records, flag the files with information on expiration
dates and limits to home and auto insurance policies, warranties, etc.

In the top drawer, put all the bills that need to be paid each
month such as credit card bills along with current bank statements. In the bottom drawer, put receipts and anything else
that you'll need to prepare your tax return.

Tax Audit   Keep at least the past seven years of tax returns and supporting documentation in the event you're audited by the IRS. Make sure you label each file clearly. Use a simple system so that you can put your fingers on the items quickly.

At least once a year, clean out your files. When an item becomes obsolete, throw it out!

In this lesson, you learned how to organize financial records. In the next lesson, you will learn how to use many of these records to prepare a budget.

BUDGETING

In this lesson, you will learn how to set up a budget, and how budgeting helps you control your finances.

A budget is a written record of your financial picture. You use a budget to record what you are spending and then set up a target or goal of how much you want to spend in the future.

Preparing your budget will provide you with insights. You'll begin to see if you spend too much in any one area. You should also start to feel more in control of your money.

GETTING STARTED

Here's what you'll need to get going:

- Calculator
- Cash receipts (three months)
- Checkbook register
- Credit card bills (three months)
- Wage statements (12 months)
- Last year's tax returns (state and federal)

Quiet Time Make sure you have time by yourself. Sort out your budget on the weekend, or while the children are in school.

WHY YOU NEED ONE

Preparing a budget allows you to see into the future and uncover some of the surprises waiting for you. When you focus on where your money is coming from and where it's going, you're able to control your finances.

Don't put off getting started. The sooner you're in charge, the better off your finances will be.

Compare your spending with how much you have coming in. With a budget, your aim is to balance out the two. If you want more than you can afford, you may have to change some of your goals.

It's usually impossible to get everything you want at once. That's why in Lesson 3 you set up a priority list. What do you want and when do you want it?

A budget in not a permanent record. Your budget will be in constant change. The budget you have when you're just out of school is different from the budget you have when you get married, buy a home, or have a baby. You change, life changes, and the budget changes.

FIGURING INCOME AND EXPENSE

Start by collecting all of the information on how much money you have coming in each month. Use the worksheet shown in figure 5.1 to help you get going.

SOURCES OF CASH	AMOUNT	TARGET	ACTUAL
Your After-Tax Salary			
Spouse's After-Tax Salary			
Work Bonus			
Interest and Dividends			
Rental Income			
Alimony & Child Support			
Social Security			
Disability Income			
Unemployment Compensation			
Pension			
Commision			
Tips (just between us)			
Other			
Total			

Figure 5.1   Monthly Income

For amounts that you don't know precisely, estimate (but always on the low side). If your goal is to increase your income, use column B to list the target amount. Use column C to keep track of how close you are to your goal. Be sure to pick a date in the future to record the actual amount of earnings.

Be Conservative   When estimating your income and expenses, always err on the low side when it comes to income and on the high side when it comes to expenses. That way, even if your estimates are off, you should still be alright.

To track expenses, pull out your checkbook register, cash receipts, and charge card bills. Categorize the expense using the worksheet in figure 5.2.

Estimate Expenses   Go back in your records for the last three months. Total the numbers in each category and then divide by three. The average number should be close enough for budgeting purposes.

Use the following list to help you find where to place miscellaneous expenses:

Other   Child care, education, business expense, contributions, alimony, and child support

Debt   School loans, credit cards, home equity, and installment loans

If your goal is to cut expenses, use column C to set your target amount and column D to begin tracking actual expense.

Stay on Target   Take a 12 column notepad and record your actual expense over the next 12 months to see how close to your target amount you stayed.

MONTHLY EXPENSE	TOTAL AMOUNT	TARGET	ACTUAL
FOOD			
Groceries			
Meals out			
Total			
CLOTHING			
Purchase			
Shoes			
Accessories			
Total			
TRANSPORTATION			
Car Payments			
Repairs and Gas			
Public Transportation			
Total			
HOUSING			
Mortgage or Rent			
Maintenance			
Utilities			
Furniture			
Total			
RECREATION			
Movies			
Television			
Clubs			
Subscriptions			
Total			
PERSONAL CARE			
Life Insurance			
Life Insurance			
Legal			
Miscellaneous			
OTHER			
TOTAL			

Figure 5.2   Average Monthly Expenses

Do the numbers seem right? Have you accounted for all the cash you spend on snacks, cigarettes, and newspapers? If you know you're spending more than the numbers show, you'll have to start writing down all your expenses.

Next, take your calculator and add all the numbers showing income and all the numbers showing expense. What's the total? Is the number positive or negative? Are you making more than you spend? Or, are you spending more than you make?

Don't panic if you're in the red. You will read about ways to balance these columns and reduce expense in Lesson 7.

 Computer Help   If you have a computer, you may want to consider using a program such as Quicken or Microsoft Money to help you prepare a cash flow statement and manage your budget.

PROJECTING AN ANNUAL BUDGET

Take a sheet of paper and make 12 columns. List your average monthly income and project the numbers out for the next 12 months. Will your income increase due to an expected second job or a raise? Do the same with expenses. Will your expenses increase because of taxes, Christmas purchases, or a vacation?

Your budget will help you see what's ahead. If you see that an upcoming expense is going to throw off your budget, you can start cutting back expenses now. When your budget's not balancing, you have only two choices—make more or spend less!

In this lesson, you learned how to collect the numbers needed to set up a budget, and how to use those numbers to help prevent financial trouble ahead. In the next lesson, you'll find out how to come up with the money you need as a cash cushion.

PLANNING FOR UPCOMING EXPENSES

In this lesson, you'll learn how to use periodic payments in order to save up for both planned and unplanned upcoming expenses.

What do you want and when do you want it? Remember, in Lesson 3 you decided what to do with your money. Now you'll see how you can pay for it.

USING PERIODIC PAYMENTS

Take a look at the worksheet shown in figure 6.1. Here's what you do. In the first column, you're going to transfer your goals from figure 3.1, listing them by order of priority. In the second column, you're going to set up a time frame for reaching your goal. Is it in one year, three years, five years, etc.?

Changes Because your finances will fluctuate, you'll most likely be making changes, so use a pencil and have a good eraser handy.

GOAL	BY WHEN	HOW MUCH	HOW MANY	PAYMENT AMOUNT

Figure 6.1 Game plan

For the third column, how much is this dream going to cost you? Fourth, figure the number of deposits you'll need to make your dream come true.

If you want "it" in five years and you're going to put money aside every month, this number would be 60 (5 years × 12 months).

And finally, how much will each payment have to be in order for you to accomplish your goal? Don't worry, it's not that hard—look at Table 6.1 for an example.

TABLE 6.1   GAME PLAN EXAMPLE

GOAL	BY WHEN	HOW MUCH	HOW MANY	PAYMENT AMOUNT
Honda Spree	May, 97	$1,200	14 months	$85.71
Pay off Visa	Jan, 98	$3,000	22 months	$136.36

The hardest part is determining how much you need to save each month. Divide how much you need by how many months until you need it. Don't take interest into account in this calculation. The rule is to keep it simple. The numbers will usually be close enough to give you the target you need.

This may be easy but where is the money going to come from?

FINDING THE MONEY

You may have heard the saying "pay yourself first." Most of the financial problems you'll ever face could be avoided if you put aside a part of each paycheck. The key is to pay yourself before you start paying your bills. You should try to set aside ten percent. There's never any money left over after the bills are paid.

Start Small   If saving ten percent is too much, try five, or four, or three. Start small, just get in the habit, and increase a little at a time.

Painless Savings   Have your savings automatically deducted from your paycheck and deposited into a savings account. What you don't see, you don't miss.

There are other ways to find more money:

- Take a second job, and save your salary
- Take in a roommate
- Don't spend your tax refund

- Stop smoking
- Save all cash gifts
- Ask for a raise
- Send in refund offers
- Sell things you don't need
- Read Lesson 7 on how to reduce expenses

However, before you start putting money away to save up for your dreams in the future, you must first deal with avoiding the nightmares.

SETTING UP AN EMERGENCY FUND

You can't avoid the unexpected such as illness or losing your job, so you better prepare for these situations by setting up an emergency fund.

 Emergency Fund   A pool of cash you can draw from (without penalty) when you need money fast. Usually kept in a savings account or other short-term investment.

When you need money for repairs or medical bills, use funds from this pool. It should be reserved for unexpected and un-avoidable financial emergencies.

How much do you need? You should have three months worth of living expenses to meet all expenses in case you can't (or won't) work. This money will cover rent, car payments, utilities, groceries, gas, and baby-sitters.

This probably sounds like a lot. But, unfortunately, you often need more. Whenever you suspect that a major change is possible—from divorce, job loss, new child, and so on—you need to increase your fund to six months of living expenses. And, you need the money where you can get it fast.

Keep your emergency fund in the bank in a basic savings account, money market account, or short-term Certificates of Deposit (CDs).

Basic Savings Account   Usually at a bank or a credit union. These are interest paying accounts with no minimum deposits or withdrawals.

Money Market Account   Savings account with higher interest and limited check writing. Often have a minimum initial deposit to open the account.

Certificate of Deposit   Earn higher interest than both savings accounts and money market accounts. They pay a guaranteed rate of return until they come due.

How do you build up an emergency fund? Make periodic payments your top priority. Every time you take money out for an emergency, you should immediately start to put it back. Your other goals will have to wait until you get your cushion back in place.

In this lesson, you learned how to go about meeting your goals through the use of periodic payments. In Lesson 7, you'll find out what to do if your spending exceeds your income.

7

WHEN YOU SPEND MORE THAN YOU MAKE

In this lesson, you'll learn how to cut back on what you're spending.

It may only happen for one month, or it may happen all the time. Either way, when your budget is in the red, you've only got two choices: earn more or spend less.

WAYS TO REDUCE EXPENSES

Impulse buying probably takes up more of your income than you realize. It's hard to have self control. No matter how you look at it, not buying something isn't nearly as much fun as having a new "thing."

ADJUSTING YOUR GOALS

There is one other option (other than making more or spending less) when you're in the red. You can change your goals. For example, instead of getting a new Jeep Wrangler at $21,000, buy the pared down version at $13,000. Or better yet, one used.

Car Buying   New cars are a poor deal. The minute you drive off the lot, the cars drop thousands of dollars in value. Buy used.

You spend less on what you want, or you put off the purchase until later. The less money you need to meet your goals, or the longer it is until you need it, the less money you'll need to spend right now.

USING CREDIT

Don't do it. Only in the strictest of emergencies should you borrow money when you're already spending more than you make.

You can't borrow your way out of debt. Declare a moratorium on credit card purchases. And stick with it.

In this lesson, you've learned how to adjust goals and reduce expenses when you find you're spending more than you make. In Lesson 8, you'll discover when it makes sense to borrow money and some of the types of loans available.

WHEN YOU SHOULD BORROW

In this lesson, you will learn some of the reasons why you should borrow money.

Since almost everything you want to buy is more expensive than you can easily afford, it's rare to find anyone who doesn't owe money.

Managing the debt associated with living in the 90s means educating and training yourself so that you never borrow needlessly.

BORROWING FOR THE RIGHT REASONS

Becoming a savvy borrower can make the difference between financial security and failure. You can help protect yourself by following these rules:

- Borrow only what you can comfortably afford to pay back

- Borrow only when the reasons are right

What are the right reasons?

- When you make significant purchases such as a house or a car
- When you need to pay for college costs
- When an unforeseen emergency occurs
- When you can buy something on sale that you know you'll need soon
- When you can pay off a higher interest rate loan with the money

On occasion, there may be another reason to borrow. You may want to borrow money to invest. You should borrow money only if you're virtually certain that the money can successfully be used to increase your wealth.

USING TEMPORARY LOANS

Sometimes, it makes sense to take out a short-term loan. These kinds of loans are considered temporary because they are usually for terms less than 12 months.

You use temporary loans when:

- You want to pay off high interest credit card debt by taking out a lower interest card
- You have an emergency
- You need to pay bills while you're waiting for payment from someone else

The key is, you don't hold onto the money for a long time.

Card Pitfalls   You can cut high interest rates by rolling debt into lower rate cards but you should be sure to read the fine print. Low rates may apply only for a short time or you may have to pay a higher rate on the transferred debt. And, you should always cancel the higher rate card to avoid further temptation.

Short-term loans come from:

- A line of credit
- Home equity loans
- Family members
- Credit cards
- Retirement plans
- Life insurance

Line of Credit   An unsecured loan usually arranged in connection with a checking account or credit card. The line has a limit. You use what you need up to that limit.

Home Equity Loan   A loan taken against the cash built up in your house. Often, this loan is tax deductible. (See Lesson 9 for more detailed information on these loans.)

Using Loans for Cars, Houses, and School

Car Loans

When you borrow money to buy a car, the car is your collateral. This means that the lender can take back the auto if you can't repay the loan. Typically, car loans are made by banks, credit unions, and car dealers.

You can borrow the money over a period of three to five years. After you make the final payment, the car is yours.

 Special Deals   Check promotions from dealers. Financing rates can sometimes drop to as low as zero percent. Be sure to read the fine print to uncover other charges.

When you're looking at terms for a car loan, assume that everything is negotiable. When you're a good credit risk, you have more bargaining power. When you're a poor credit risk, unfortunately, you won't be able to get the best rates.

Mortgages

Unless you've been left a large trust fund or won the lottery, you'll most likely have to take out a mortgage to buy your home. Fortunately, taking out a mortgage is one debt that makes sense to carry.

The biggest benefit to taking out most home mortgages is that
the interest you pay (on mortgages up to $1,000,000 and
home equity loans up to $100,000) is deductible from your
income taxes. Essentially, this means the government is help-
ing you pay off the cost of the mortgage. (How much help? If
you're in the 28 percent federal tax bracket, interest on a 30-
year $100,000 mortgage at 80 percent could save you over
$2,000 in the first year.)

 True Cost   Don't lose track of the true cost of a
mortgage. You still have to pay in one dollar for
each average 28 cent break the IRS gives you.

The best way to find a mortgage is to start comparison shopping by looking at ads in your local paper, calling local banks,
and checking with mortgage brokers. You can also ask your
real estate agent for recommendations and ask friends who
have recently bought a home where they got their mortgage.

 Mortgage Broker   These are the services that will
help you find the best mortgage for a fee. If you
have good credit, they may charge up to two percent of the amount you're borrowing. Those with
poor credit will usually pay up to ten percent.

Once you've decided which lender to use, you need to know
the types of mortgages to consider.

- **Conventional Mortgage.** Most conventional
  mortgages require that you put down 20 percent of
  the purchase price. The remaining amount is fi-
  nanced at *fixed* rates over a 15- or 30-year period.

Mortgage Length   You should use a 30-year mortgage versus a 15-year one. Monthly payments will be smaller. When you have extra funds, you can make larger payments to pay the mortgage off early. Then, if you have a cash crunch, you can drop down to the smaller required monthly payment.

- **Adjustable Rate Mortgages (ARMs).** These feature a varying rate of interest that is usually tied to the government's prime rate or one-year treasury bills. Usually, the rate changes once a year. Look at your ARM's "cap," which is the maximum amount of interest charged. Do some calculations to make sure you will be able to pay the maximum monthly payment.

 The Trouble with ARMs   They make it hard to set a budget. Interest rates can become too high and you'll end up paying a lot more interest than you may have hoped.

- **VA and FHA Mortgages.** These let you borrow more of the cost of the home and make a smaller downpayment. With VA loans, you must be a veteran to qualify. For FHA mortgages, the home must meet some strict qualifications such as bringing electrical plumbing and heating with state safety standards.

Assumable Mortgages FHA and VA mortgages can often be passed on to the next buyer. The low interest rates can be kept and closing costs eliminated.

When you're applying for a mortgage, you will be required to provide the following:

- The completed application
- Your social security number
- A copy of the contract of sale
- A survey of your property
- A list of what you own and what you owe
- Verification of all income
- Account numbers and addresses of your financial institutions
- Tax return for the past two years

SCHOOL

With the average annual cost at many colleges well over $11,000, finding money to pay these expenses can be overwhelming. Unless your child is fortunate enough to win a full or partial scholarship, you should assume that you'll have to borrow some money for college costs.

Borrowing money for you or your children to go to school is, without a doubt, a reason to borrow money. You should view a college loan as an investment with earning power.

College Help   Go to your local library and spend some time researching which scholarships and grants you may be able to use. By doing this yourself, you won't have to pay a search service for the same information.

Once you exhaust all the possibilities for private and publicly funded scholarships, you should look for any federal or state loans and grants. Interest on these loans is usually low.

 Work-study grants   Many colleges offer campus jobs to students. Students either receive a salary or the earnings can be deducted from the cost of tuition.

Students don't need a credit history or collateral to borrow from the federal or state governments. However, parents will have their credit histories reviewed. Also, the interest rate for loans taken out by parents will be higher than on loans made directly to the students. (For more help, read the *10 Minute Guide to Paying for College* by William D. VanDusen.)

In this lesson, you learned when it makes sense to take out a loan and some of the types of loans available. In the next lesson, you'll learn more about where to go to borrow money.

WHERE TO BORROW MONEY

In this lesson, you will learn about the various lenders you can borrow money from.

Now that you know when it makes sense to borrow, you need to know where you can get a loan. Almost anyone can get a loan, but the cost of the loan varies depending on where you get it.

If you're sure that borrowing makes sense, then you also want to be sure to borrow wisely. For example, you should not go to a loan shark.

 Loan Sharks People who lend money at very high rates of interest. Loan sharks don't follow any federal truth-in-lending laws.

Always shop for a loan. Talk to two or three lenders when you need money. Ask the lenders to explain the features and differences of all the loans available to you.

Here's a look at some of the best sources of loans.

CREDIT UNIONS, BANKS, AND SAVINGS AND LOANS

Always start at a financial institution where you're already known. If you have an account at a local bank or credit union, start there.

Credit unions usually make lower rate loans to their members. You have to be a member to qualify, but it's usually worth the cost of joining.

 Membership   To find a credit union in your community, write The Credit Union National Association, at P.O. Box 431, Madison, WI 53701.

Also, credit unions often feature more flexibility in their repayment schedules than a bank. In addition, in the years credit unions are profitable, they often distribute surplus earnings to members, either as a dividend or as a rebate of loan interest.

Credit unions typically offer the following types of loans:

- Home improvement
- Auto loans
- Personal
- Education

Banks are somewhat less flexible than credit unions, but can still be a good deal, and you should check with one or two while shopping for a loan.

Banks offer these loans:

- Home
- Home improvement
- Auto
- Personal

Savings and Loan associations (S&Ls) work like credit unions. As with credit unions, loans from an S&L can cost less than a bank loan. Also, you don't have to be a member of an S&L to take advantage of these rates.

S&Ls have the following types of loans:

- Home
- Home improvement
- Auto
- Personal
- Education

LIFE INSURANCE

If you have any older cash value life insurance policies such as whole life, universal, or variable insurance, you may have a source of ready cash to meet your needs.

You borrow the money against the cash value of the policy and pay it back to yourself. You write the check to the insurance company, but the money is deposited back into your cash account.

Caution   Remember, when you take a loan against your life insurance, the amount of the loan that is not repaid will reduce the total money your beneficiaries will get when you die.

Beneficiary   The person (one or more) you name in your insurance policy to receive the proceeds when you die.

Usually, life insurance loans charge a low rate of interest. Still, you should read the small print on your policy to be sure you understand your policy's rules.

COMPANY RETIREMENT PLANS

Company Sponsored Retirement Plans   Often called 401(k) plans, profit sharing plans, or thrift plans.

These plans can be excellent sources of loans, if you use the plans wisely. Check with your benefits department to see whether your plan permits loans. Not all plans do.

The good news about taking a loan from your retirement plans is that you pay the interest back into your own account. The bad news is, while you have money out as a loan, you could be losing out on higher earnings if the investments do well.

Here are some common rules on retirement plan withdrawals:

- You must repay most loans over five years, unless the money is used to buy a house. Then, the loan can usually be as long as 30 years.

- You may need your spouse's approval to take the loan.

- You can only borrow up to 50 percent or up to $50,000 of the money in your plan, whichever is less.

- Sometimes, the money can only be used to cover educational expenses or to buy a house.

 Job Loss   If you leave your job, you usually have to pay back the loan within a few weeks. If you don't pay it back, the amount you still owe can be taxed as a premature withdrawal if you're under age 59 1/2.

FAMILY LOANS

Your family can be a source of cash when you need a loan. When no one else will approve your loan, family members often will lend you some money.

With family loans, you don't have to go through a credit check and interest rates are frequently low.

Note   A written document that details the terms of a loan.

To avoid stress if you borrow from a family member, you should immediately set up a repayment schedule. Spell everything out in writing and sign the document. Give everyone involved a copy.

Remember, if you borrow more than $10,000, you must be charged a reasonable rate of interest or the IRS will consider the loan a gift. This could result in tax liability in the future. The IRS updates its "reasonable" rate of interest periodically, so you should check with an accountant to find out what the current rate is.

Here are guidelines of what you should say in the note to your family:

- How much you're borrowing
- How long you'll take to repay
- What your monthly payments will be
- What interest rate you'll pay

Keep Copies   Keep a copy of your loan agreement in a safe place, such as a fireproof safe or safe deposit box.

OTHER TYPES OF LOANS

There are a few other loans that may make sense. They are as follows:

- **Home Equity.** These loans allow you to borrow from the equity of your home. Often, banks let you use special credit cards or checks that let you tap immediately into the value of your home. You pay back the loan in installments. Rates are adjustable, and having an equity line open often carries an annual fee, whether you use it or not.

 Home Security   When you use a home equity line of credit, your home is on the line. If you don't pay back the loan, you could lose your home.

- **Pawn Shops.** These businesses have an official name. Collateral loan companies may look like junk shops and bargain bins. You take in your valuables and get a loan based on what the company thinks they're worth. When you repay the money you owe, you get your items back. Otherwise, the company can keep them to resell to someone else.

 Negotiate   Pawnbrokers always start off by offering low prices so you should negotiate until you come to an agreement on price.

In this lesson, you learned some of the choices you have when borrowing money. In the next lesson, you will learn when it doesn't make sense to borrow.

10

WHEN IT DOESN'T MAKE SENSE TO BORROW

In this lesson, you will learn when it doesn't make sense to borrow money along with some common reasons people often get into trouble with borrowing.

Borrowing money is simply using someone else's cash to get what you need or want.

There's a big difference between spending some of the money you earn on necessities and supporting a lifestyle beyond your means.

LIFESTYLE CHOICES

The lifestyle you choose today is going to have a major impact on the rest of your future.

The following are some examples to guide you away from inappropriate borrowing. You should never borrow money when:

- You're in danger of losing your job

- You stretch out loans for years, allowing interest payments to drain your savings

- You borrow to support poor spending habits

- You aren't sure you'll have the money to repay a loan as promised

- You're going through major personal changes like separation, divorce, or death of a loved one

BORROWING YOUR WAY OUT OF DEBT

The idea seems simple enough—you take out a loan in order to pay off older debt. It used to be called "robbing Peter to pay Paul."

Here are some of the ways people tend to borrow themselves out of debt:

- Take out a new credit card to pay off an old balance

- Take out a consolidation loan

- Use a home equity loan to finance debt payment

Borrowing your way out of debt can be dangerous to your financial peace of mind.

Be Careful If you take out a lower interest rate credit card to pay off the balance of a higher interest card, be sure to cancel the old account. If you don't, you may be tempted to run up both cards to their limits, and end up in worse shape than you were before. Not only will you have the new card to pay off, but the old one as well.

Cancel   Cut up the credit cards you no longer want and send them back to the company to officially close the account.

Occasionally, it makes sense to borrow money to retire old debt. (For more information see the section on refinancing in Lesson 17.)

Remember, if you need to borrow money to pay off debts you already have, then you probably already owe too much money.

Buying What You Don't Need

Buying what you don't need is wasteful. And borrowing money to buy what you don't need makes no sense.

One of the greatest reasons for unnecessary debt is the purchase of items on impulse.

Particularly, if you have little willpower, spend your free time away from stores so that you don't overspend.

In this lesson, you have learned some of the reasons it doesn't make sense to borrow money. In the next lesson, you will learn how to establish credit.

ESTABLISHING CREDIT

In this lesson, you will learn how to establish credit of your own.

Building and keeping a good credit rating is one of the most important financial moves you'll ever make. It may take a little time, but it's worth it.

Remember, when you start to build your credit history, this record will be used for years to determine how much you can borrow and what rate you'll pay on loans. The better your rating, the better your loan terms.

Credit Rating   The score used by creditors to determine whether an applicant will be given credit.

Negotiate   When you have a superior credit rating, ask for better loan terms such as a lower interest rate and a longer term for the loan period of time.

Once your credit is approved, you'll have the advantage of using your credit to make life easier.

ADVANTAGES OF A GOOD CREDIT RATING

- It allows you "peace of mind." If a financial emergency comes along, you'll be able to get the money you need to take care of it.

- It gives you the freedom to buy expensive items without having to pay for them up front.

- It makes it easier to go shopping without having to carry a lot of cash.

- It makes record keeping easier. When you use a credit card for purchases, you'll get a single statement detailing what you bought and what you spent.

 Employees   How you manage your credit may affect your future job searches. Many employers check on the credit worthiness of potential employees.

WHAT CREDITORS LOOK FOR

Most lenders are looking for the same basic information. Figure 11.1 illustrates what you can expect to find on a credit application.

APPLICANT

Last Name   First Name   Middle Int.

_____   _____   _____

Street Address State   Zip Code

_____   _____   _____

Rent ___ Own ___   How long at this address _____

Cost of home _____   Mortgage holder _____

Current value _____   Balance owing _____

Monthly rent _____   Monthly mortgage _____

       Former address if less
than 3 years at current address _____

Marital status   Single _____   Married _____   Divorced _____

Social security no. _____ Birth date _____

OCCUPATION AND INCOME

Employer   Occupation

_____   _____

Employer's address _____

Empl. phone _____ Date of empl. (mo/yr) _____

Annual Salary _____

Previous employer

if less than 3 yr. _____

Additional income _____

ACCOUNTS

Type	Name and location	Acct No.	Balance
Checking	_____	_____	_____
Savings	_____	_____	_____
S&L/CU	_____	_____	_____

DEBTS

Type	Name/location	Acct No.	Balance	Mo. Pmt.
Mortgage	_____	_____	_____	_____
Auto	_____	_____	_____	_____
Credit card	_____	_____	_____	_____
Credit Union	_____	_____	_____	_____
Other	_____	_____	_____	_____

Figure 11.1   Sample credit application

Fraud   Be honest on your application. If you lie, your application may be rejected, and you may be subject to legal penalties for fraud.

Your information is often cross-checked with your credit report and your employer is often called to verify your salary.

Past problems   If you have had credit problems in the past, don't try to hide them. If you voluntarily disclose the information, you'll have the chance to explain the circumstances in your own words.

If your information is acceptable to the creditors, you'll be given a high rating, and your application will be approved. If your rating is low, you'll be turned down.

Here is a list of what creditors look for:

- You own your own home
- You've lived at your current residence five years or more
- You have a savings account
- You have a stable job
- You have a responsible job title
- You have high income with low debt
- You have a good record with other creditors (prompt payments, loan payoffs)
- You have good credit references

This list can be divided into the "Three Cs" of evaluating credit. They are: Character, Capacity, and Collateral.

Character How responsible you are about paying your bills. Do you pay on time, or do you often pay more than 30 days late?

Capacity Your ability to pay back a loan. This is reflected by how much money you earn and what you currently owe.

Collateral Security for the lender if you don't pay back the money. A car, for example, is the collateral for an auto loan.

SETTING UP YOUR CREDIT HISTORY

People who pay cash are "invisible" in today's credit world. It's important to have credit in your own name.

You'll need a credit history for reasons other than borrowing money. For example, you'll need it for routine matters such as having the utilities connected in your home.

Your Own Name Be sure to establish credit in your own name, using your own social security number. If all your credit is established in your spouse's name, you may have difficulty establishing credit on your own if you should divorce or your spouse dies.

If you're getting credit for the first time, you'll understand the saying "it takes credit to get credit." Creditors review your application and compare it to your credit report. If that report doesn't exist, you may get turned down.

The first step is to begin building your credibility:

- Let your family help. Get a family member to co-sign on a loan. However, don't take advantage of your family and be sure to pay off the loan on your own.

- Build a relationship with your local bank, and apply for a small loan. Follow the monthly payment schedule precisely.

- Check out groups or organizations such as alumni organizations, auto clubs, and unions to see if they offer credit cards to members. Use the cards carefully. Only charge small amounts and pay back the monthly minimum each month until the account is clear.

- Apply for a department store charge card. Often, stores are more liberal than other credit card issuers. Pay what you owe when the bill comes.

- Apply at your credit union. Because the loan committee usually consists of people who work at your company, you don't have to prove your character to them.

If you have trouble getting accepted for credit, you should check with the credit bureau that rejected you. There may be incorrect information in your file.

FINDING OUT HOW YOU RATE

If you frequently get preapproved credit card applications, the chances are good that you've got a sound credit rating.

However, it could be that you live in the right area, or that you graduated from the right school, or just got married. The promotion department of credit card companies get mailing lists from wedding announcements, real estate reports, yearbooks, and even tax records.

You obtain your credit rating from the credit bureaus. These bureaus collect, organize, and distribute your financial records to credit card companies, banks, stores, and finance companies.

To get a copy of your credit report, send a letter with the following information:

- Your name (and any other names you've used)

- Your current address

- Any older addresses if you've lived at your current home less than five years

- Your social security number

- Your birthdate

Request a copy of your credit report. Send a check along with your request for the amount of the processing fee.

Periodic Review   Even if you have no reason to believe there's a smear on your record, you should review your credit history every few years to make sure your information is accurate. Errors can be corrected by submitting a letter to the credit bureau explaining the situation (find out how this is done in Lesson 23).

Here are the names and addresses of the three major credit reporting services:

TRW Credit Data
505 City Parkway West, Suite 110
Orange, CA 92613-5450

Trans Union Credit Information Company
444 North Michigan Avenue
Chicago, IL 60611

CBI/Equifax
5501 Peachtree Dunwoody Road, Suite 600
Atlanta, GA 30356

When in Doubt, Ask   Ask your banker or a local department store to give you the names and addresses of the credit-reporting agencies that serve your area.

In this lesson, you have learned how to establish credit and check your credit report. In the next lesson, you will learn how to use that credit wisely.

12

CREDIT CARDS

In this lesson, you will learn how to get the best value on your credit cards and how to use them responsibly.

Today, you can charge almost everything on a credit card. Using a card is painless. The hard part comes when you have to pay the bill in the future.

FINDING OUT IF YOU USE YOUR CARDS TOO MUCH

If you're having difficulty managing your credit card debt, you probably don't have enough self-control. Cards offer convenience and safety, but you can quickly get trapped in your safety net if you're not constantly on the alert for trouble.

Here are some of the warning signs indicating that you have too much credit card debt:

- You use one card to make payments on another.

- Your cards are at their limits.

- You tend to collect cash from friends in restaurants, and then put the tab on your card.

- You use your card just to get the rewards such as flight miles, cash rebates, credit toward a new car, etc.

- You only pay the minimum due on your balance and your balance keeps rising each month.

- You hide the credit card bills from your spouse.

- You have no idea what you've charged until you get the monthly bill.

If none, or one or two, of the statements apply to you, then you are in sound credit card shape. However, you should still check the list every so often to make sure you're not getting into trouble.

However, if several signs apply to you, you're either in over your head or headed toward trouble soon. It's time to get back in control.

KICKING THE HABIT

The first, and often the hardest, step is to put away your cards and keep them out of your wallet. Next, you've got to re-double your self-control to keep from pulling the cards out again.

GETTING YOURSELF OUT OF DEBT

Record Charges   Always write down the amount of your charge card purchases in your checkbook register and deduct what you charge from your balance. This keeps the total handy, and helps you avoid letting the balance build to an amount you're not able to pay off in full at the end of the month.

Use Color   Write your charges in a different color ink to draw your attention to the amount.

Once you've stopped using the cards, you must make a plan for paying off your debt. Use the following strategies:

- Consolidate your credit card debt onto one lower-rate card.

- Renegotiate with your own card company for lower rates (see the suggestions below).

- Make more than the minimum payments each month.

- Cut back on discretionary spending. Use the extra cash to pay down your card balances.

- Contact a budgeting and credit counseling service (see Lesson 17).

When you've stopped using credit cards, you'll probably find you don't need them as much. But, if you often use them when you travel to rent cars or pay hotel bills, consider using a debit card.

Debit cards look just like credit cards but they have key differences. Debit cards are backed by your own bank account and work like checks. When you use them, the amount of the purchase is automatically deducted from your bank account. You can't exceed your limit and, because it's your own money, you have no interest to pay.

The advantages of debit cards include the following:

- They're easy to use.

- The money is withdrawn directly from your account.

- They reduce the temptation to overspend.

The disadvantages of debit cards include the following:

- Most don't offer any "float time," so your money has to be available at the time of purchase. (With credit cards, you usually have 30 days before the bill comes due.)

- They don't help build credit references because you're not paying off a loan.

- Some have transaction fees ranging from $.50 to $2.

- They have no $50 loss limit protection. If your card is stolen, the thieves have access to your whole account.

REDUCING YOUR INTEREST RATE

It's always better to pay your card balances off in full each month, but if you don't (or can't), then you should try to lower the interest rates you're paying. Lowering the interest rate you pay on your card balance can save you hundreds of dollars each year and allow you to repay your bills in less time.

What you need to get started:

- The names and numbers of your credit card companies
- The names and numbers of several other banks
- Some knowledge of what other banks are offering (look in the paper or collect the applications that come in the mail)
- A good credit rating

Begin by calling up your current card issuer. Ask to speak to the supervisor or manager. If you have received other credit card offers featuring a lower rate, tell your issuer. Ask them to meet the lower rate or threaten to move your balance elsewhere.

If you've been a good customer, your card issuer will probably lower its rates. And while you're on the phone, ask whether your annual service fee can be eliminated as well.

If your card company won't lower its rates, then switch. Find another card with low interest and move your balance over.

Read   Always check on how long the low introductory rates will last. Make sure you have your balance paid off before the interest rates go up.

Caution   When you roll your card balances onto a new card, be sure to cancel your old account. Don't get trapped into letting the old balance creep back up.

If you don't receive low interest rate applications, you need to find them yourself:

- Read advertisements in the newspapers and magazines
- Ask your friends about offers they've received
- Check with your bank, S&L, and credit union

Once you've found a lower rate card, you can usually move your old card balance in one of two ways. You can use the convenience checks—blank checks provided by your new bank when you first set up your account—offered by the new card. Or, you can ask your new creditor to pay off your old balance directly.

PROTECTING YOURSELF

With the convenience of credit cards comes responsibility. You have to protect yourself against others using your cards.

Protect yourself by following this advice:

- Tear up all carbons when you take your credit receipts
- Try to keep your eye on your card at all times
- Never give your number over the phone—unless you're the one that placed the call
- Always compare bills with receipts to check for errors
- Sign cards as soon as you receive them
- Cut up and return all unwanted cards to the issuer

- Report a lost card as soon as you can

- Never sign a blank receipt

For specific problems, you may have to contact your card issuer directly. If that doesn't get you the results you want, send a letter to the appropriate credit card server listed as follows:

American Express
Public Relations
American Express Tower
World Financial Center
New York, NY 10285-3130

MasterCard International
Public Relations
888 Seventh Avenue
New York, NY 10106

Visa
Public Relations
P.O. Box 8999
San Francisco, CA 94128

Discover
External Communications
2 World Trade Center, 70th Floor
New York, NY 10048

In this lesson, you learned about managing your credit card debt. In the next lesson, you will learn how to tell if you have problems with other kinds of debt.

13

HOW TO TELL IF YOU'RE IN TROUBLE WITH DEBT

In this lesson, you'll learn to recognize the signs of trouble and understand the guidelines for acceptable limits of debt.

Getting in over your head in debt doesn't happen overnight. In turn, repairing the damage will take time, commitment, and a lot of resolve.

To find out if you're too weighed down by debt, review this checklist. (The checklist in the last lesson helped you determine if you had a problem with your credit card debt. This checklist covers all types of installment debt.)

SIGNS OF TROUBLE

_____You worry about money frequently

_____You have trouble making house or rent payment on time

_____You take out new loans before old ones are paid off

_____You need to postdate checks

_____You put off seeing the doctor because you can't afford the visit

_____You've frequently bounced checks

_____You have to work overtime to make ends meet

_____You routinely get calls from creditors about unpaid or late bills

_____You pay half your bills one month and half the next

_____You have to dip into savings and investments to meet your bills

_____You pay bills with money ear-marked for another purpose

_____You've been denied credit

If you check off one or two items, you're probably all right today but may be headed for trouble in the future. Even if none of the items applies to you now, you should periodically review the danger signals so you can avoid problems in the future. However, if you have checked off most of the items, then you're already in a crisis situation.

DETERMINING WHAT YOU OWE

The first step toward gaining control of your debts is to figure out how much you owe to each creditor. Begin by making a list of everyone to whom you owe money (excluding mortgages). Write down banks, credit card companies, department stores, credit unions, retirement plans, and all other sources of installment debt you are presently carrying.

Installment Debt Money you borrow at once but pay back in set amounts on a regular schedule.

Next, put down the dollar amount it will take to pay off your obligations.

Bills Collect your credit card bills, loan statements, and paycheck stubs. Have everything together before you sit down to complete the worksheet in figure 13.1.

Creditor	Loan Balance	Monthly Payment
TOTAL		

Figure 13.1 Tracking debt

FINDING THE ACCEPTABLE LIMITS

After you've recorded your debt obligations, you can begin to analyze the figures.

Everyone's comfort level will be somewhat different, but you should use the "20 percent rule" as a benchmark.

20 Percent Rule   20 percent is usually considered an acceptable debt/equity ratio.

Start by finding your total debt-to-income ratio. You can easily see how your actual monthly payments relate to your monthly take-home pay by dividing the payments by your average after-tax monthly income.

Now, you'll want to find your acceptable limits of debt. To do this, take your annual take-home pay and divide it by 12.

Next, take the resulting number and multiply by 20 percent (.20). For example, if your annual salary is $35,000, you would divide that by 12, which equals $2,917. Then, you'd multiply $2,917 by 20 percent, which equals $583.

Does your total debt exceed the tolerable limit of 20 percent of annual after-tax income? If it does, assume you're headed for trouble.

You can also use the following table to quickly determine your 20 percent income-to-debt ratio:

Annual Income	Monthly Take-Home Pay	20 Percent Debt Limit Per Month
$20,000	$1,667	$333
$25,000	$2,083	$417
$30,000	$2,500	$500
$35,000	$2,917	$583
$40,000	$3,333	$667
$45,000	$3,750	$750
$50,000	$4,167	$833
$55,000	$4,583	$917
$60,000	$5,000	$1,000

If you're just under or right at 20 percent, you should be all right. Still, you should watch your spending to make sure you don't purchase something that will bump you over the limit.

If you're at:

- 20–35 percent, start cutting back.

- 35–50 percent, you're in the danger zone. You already have too much debt and need to cut back immediately. At this point, you may even need to talk to a credit counselor if you feel that you can't handle your finances on your own.

Ideally, you should keep your debt under 15 percent. At this manageable level, you'll have greater flexibility in your financial decisions than when a large part of income is going toward repaying your debt.

Reminder   The previously mentioned limits are not the guidelines used by creditors. Many creditors will lend substantially more than average consumers can comfortably afford to repay.

Lenders Ratio   Many lenders follow the 28/36 percent rule when evaluating debt/income. This means total housing debt plus insurance plus taxes should not exceed 28 percent of gross income. Total monthly debt (housing plus all other debt) should not exceed 36 percent of monthly gross income.

In this lesson, you learned how to recognize the warning signs of a debt crisis and how to determine if you are carrying too much debt. In the next lesson, you will learn how to find the road back.

14

GETTING OUT FROM UNDER DEBT

In this lesson, you will learn some of the crucial first steps to help get you get out of debt.

If you've turned directly to this chapter, you already know you need help with your debt. Don't despair—there are strategies that will enable you to regain control over your debt.

Admitting that you need to change your habits is a crucial step toward correcting the problem. In fact, it's often the most difficult step.

There are many things you can do to get back on the road to financial security. While some of the steps are painful, others won't seem too difficult at all.

TAKING THE FIRST STEP

The first step in getting out of debt is quite simple. In fact, it may appear far too simple. You have to stop borrowing money to buy things. Anything. And you need to do it immediately!

GETTING TO THE ROOT OF YOUR PROBLEM

Carrying too much debt can be a sign of deeper problems. If you can uncover the reasons why you overspend, you're on the way to being able to cut back on your spending. You'll have to spend some time thinking about why you spend too much.

Here are some common causes of overspending:

- Depression
- Family problems
- Job stress
- Boredom

Are you depressed or in a bad relationship? If you are, you need to talk to a counselor instead of spending money you don't have. Don't tell yourself you can't afford the counseling. You can't afford not to! You don't want to spend yourself into foreclosure or bankruptcy, do you?

Counseling If you need a counselor but don't have any money, call the Family Service agency in your area, which can provide counseling on a low- or no-fee basis.

If your job isn't going well, start looking for something else. If you've got time on your hands, fill it. Take a job, volunteer your time at a hospital or school, just do something productive—something that doesn't involve spending money.

CHANGING YOUR HABITS

Often, building up debt is nothing more than a bad habit. You see what you want and you buy it, without giving any thought to the consequences.

In order to improve your financial position, you need to change your habits and spending patterns.

To replace bad habits with good ones, try these steps toward changing your behavior:

1. Take a look at your lifestyle. Do you live beyond your means? If you do, you need to stick to a stricter budget.

2. Bring your spending under control. Learn to stop spending more than you make. You must stop getting in over your head.

3. Increase your income. Use the extra cash to pay off your debt.

4. Work on setting and prioritizing your financial goals.

5. Develop a game plan for meeting your goals in advance. Don't pay for them "after-the-fact" with your charge card.

Once you understand what has caused your problem, you can start using some techniques to bring down your burden of debt.

Applying the Rollover Technique

If you have money that you can now use to begin paying off debt, try this method of applying extra income to retire high interest debt.

To begin, determine the largest amount of cash not earmarked for other bills in your budget. Calculate the amount that you can comfortably afford to pay toward debt each month. Apply that amount to the highest interest debt and pay only required minimums on all the others.

Keep applying extra cash each month until you pay off the account with the highest interest. Then, you can begin concentrating on the next highest, and so on.

 Savings   Don't deplete your savings account to pay off debt. You should always keep a cash reserve of three to six months expenses in case of an emergency.

Across the top of your worksheet, list the creditors that charge the highest interest, and show what that interest rate is.

Write in, under each creditor, the amount you'll be paying on the account. Remember, always add extra money to the highest interest balance only.

Add lines and columns on another sheet of paper if needed. When you pay off the most expensive creditor, continue applying that amount to the monthly balance paid to the second most expensive creditor, until they too are paid off.

This technique is known as "folding over" and should be continued until all creditors are paid in full.

 Takes Time   This process will take time, so you will need to have patience. Your reward will be greater financial security and peace of mind.

In this lesson, you learned to take the first steps toward regaining control of your debt. In the next lesson, you will learn techniques for borrowing money to pay off your outstanding debt.

Borrowing Money to Pay Off Debt

In this lesson, you will learn about the various loans you can use to pay off outstanding debt.

When you're indebted to several creditors and have to pay the loans at different interest rates and varying schedules, it can get confusing and downright expensive. Sometimes, it makes sense to roll a number of high-interest debt obligations into one lower monthly payment.

Consolidating Loans

Debt consolidation loans can be a useful tool to bring down monthly payments. Having a single monthly payment makes bill paying less complicated and easier to manage.

There are many ways to consolidate bills. Some are fairly easy, such as moving credit card balances into a lower rate card. And some will take effort and time.

Before you consider this option, ask yourself:

- Will the consolidation loan reduce my overall debt load?

- Am I going to stop buying on credit?

Of course, the answer to both questions should be yes. If it isn't, then a consolidation loan may not be the best choice for you.

 Borrowed Money   The money you borrow to pay off bills is not extra income. Never consider this cash as a source of surplus spending money.

Borrowing money to pay creditors takes discipline and determination. You have to be certain you're going to have the self-control it takes to keep from spending the money somewhere else.

 Co-signer   If you're already in financial trouble, you may not have much luck taking out any new loans, even if the loans would lower your overall monthly bills. Finding someone to co-sign on a loan may be your best, and only, option.

Until your new loan is paid back in full, you must not continue to accumulate debt. If you do, you'll only end up in worse financial shape than you were before.

Promise   It may help to make a promise to repay the funding to someone else before you assume any new debt. Put it in writing to document your pledge.

There are many types of loan consolidations available. Here are some of the best choices along with the pros and cons of each option.

HOME EQUITY LOANS

Home equity loans help you reduce the interest rate you pay on your loans. With home equity loans, you put up your house as security for repayment.

Home Equity   The cash value built up in your home. It is usually 50 to 80 percent of the market value minus any outstanding mortgage.

Here's how these loans work. They're a line of credit against the built-up equity in your home. If you don't tap into the money available, you pay nothing. You pay interest only on the amount of money you withdraw.

Here are some of the advantages of home equity loans:

- Interest on loans up to $100,000 is usually deductible on your income taxes.

Tax Savings Never take out any loan just for tax saving purposes. Remember, you have to pay one dollar for each 28 cents (assuming you're in the 28 percent tax bracket) of deductibility.

- Interest rates are generally lower than on credit cards. For example, the monthly payments on $5,000 at 18 percent would equal $75. If you paid off the balance with a lower interest home equity loan at 11 percent, your savings would be around $350 a year.

- They're easy to use; you just write checks.

Now for the disadvantages:

- You're putting your home at risk. With a home equity loan, your house serves as collateral. If you default on the loan, your house can be taken by the bank.

- They often carry high minimum loan amounts, usually $5,000. This often makes it impractical to borrow smaller amounts.

- If you continue to run up debt, you'll be in worse financial shape than you were before.

- Home equity loans usually feature longer terms than other loans. Therefore, you may end up paying more interest in the long run.

If you're going to use these loans, be sure to shop around for the best deal. Different banks offer lower rates and better terms.

BILL CONSOLIDATION LOANS

There are basically two types of bill consolidation loans:

- **The personal unsecured loan**—The financial institution pays the loan directly to you. Then you control the repayment to your creditors.

- **The bill consolidation loan**—With these loans, the financial institution writes a loan for the amount of debt, cancels your old accounts, and makes payments to creditors on your behalf.

Consolidation loans allow you to combine debt into one loan at interest rates from a few points above prime to more than 40 percent.

 Prime Rate   The lowest commercial interest rate available.

While these loans can be helpful, you should only consider them when you can lower the rates of interest paid on *all* the bills you want to consolidate. Use the following chart to help you organize all the important information about your current debt.

CREDITOR/TYPE OF LOAN	BALANCE	INTEREST
_____	$_____	_____%
_____	$_____	_____%
_____	$_____	_____%
_____	$_____	_____%
_____	$_____	_____%
_____	$_____	_____%
_____	$_____	_____%
Total	$_____	_____%

When you review your information, make sure you don't roll any debts that are already at a low rate of interest into your consolidation loan. For instance, if the consolidation loan is at 11 percent and your credit card company is charging 10.25 percent, it wouldn't make sense to roll that balance into the higher interest loan.

Here is the primary advantage of consolidation loans:

- They allow you to take large monthly payments and spread them out over time, usually two to three years.

Here are the disadvantages:

- Because these loans tend to be made to people already experiencing credit trouble, you may have a difficult time finding a finance company willing to extend a loan at reasonable rates. If that happens, you should find a co-signer to help guarantee your note.

- You forget that you're in trouble and you let your charge cards go right back up to their limits.

- You turn interest-free loans into interest-bearing ones. For example, doctors usually don't charge interest on the unpaid portion of their bills. If you took the balance you owed a doctor and rolled it into a consolidation loan, you would have turned an interest-free loan into a interest-bearing one.

- They can stigmatize the borrower as a poor credit risk.

 Avoid bill-paying services that advertise they can erase a poor credit record While these services may pay your bills each month, they don't refinance them and they don't erase your poor credit rating. That takes time and effort on your part.

LIFE INSURANCE LOANS

Another type of loan that's often overlooked is a loan from cash value life insurance policies.

Read the fine print of your policy to find out the interest rates. Often, the interest rates are quite low. You can pay back the money at your own pace, rather than adhering to a preset schedule.

However, if you don't pay the loan back before you die, the balance is subtracted from your death benefit.

In this lesson, you learned about loan options to pay off debt. In the next lesson, you'll find out how to negotiate with your creditors.

16

NEGOTIATING WITH CREDITORS

In this lesson, you will learn about the options available through creditors if you're working on managing your debt problems.

If you've made every effort on your part (refer to Lesson 14) and you still can't comfortably or practically afford to pay back your debt, it's time to contact your creditors.

Calling Creditors Don't call too soon. Call to work out a repayment schedule only when you're certain you won't be able to keep up payments. Rescheduling payments will go on your credit record.

DEVELOPING REPAYMENT PLANS

Most banks and lending institutions don't want to repossess cars or foreclose on homes. They just want their money. Sometimes that means they'll be willing to accept payments at a different rate than the original terms of the loan.

Names and Numbers Collect the names and numbers of those you need to contact.

While you shouldn't call too soon, neither should you call too late. Don't wait until the creditors contact you. Call as soon as you know there is a problem.

You'll stand a better chance of negotiating if you call before you get threatened with collection.

When you call, follow these steps:

1. Ask for the supervisor.

2. Explain your situation.

3. Ask how a new plan can be arranged to reduce your monthly payments.

You may need to set up an appointment to meet in person. Here's what you'll need to take with you:

- Your budget

- An idea of what you can pay your creditors each month

- An alternative payment offer

WHAT YOU CAN EXPECT

While there is no guarantee your creditor will agree to a specific plan, you should still know the various options that are generally available when you try to restructure your loans. Here are some examples of what your lender may do:

- Grant you a temporary reduction in the amount you pay
- Delay payments until you get back on your feet
- Waive any late charges
- Extend the length of the loan to reduce monthly payments
- Let you pay interest only for a while
- Let you pay just principal temporarily
- Lower the interest by refinancing

Be honest with yourself. Don't commit to something you know you can't or won't do. By all means, once you've worked out a repayment plan you must stick with it to the letter, or you'll be left with disastrous marks on your credit history for years.

 Names Always get the name and number of the person that agrees to the new plan. You may need it later to confirm your conversation.

Once you've come to an agreement, be sure to send a letter detailing your discussion, and request that the creditor send you written confirmation of the new arrangement.

About a week after your initial call, check back to be sure your creditors have:

- Revised your payments to show the new schedule
- Reduced the balance of all former accounts to zero

What to Tell Them

Answer all questions but don't volunteer more information than you're asked for.

Tell the creditors the following:

- You are making every effort to form a workable re-payment schedule that will allow you to pay off all of your debts.

- That you have stopped adding to your debt.

- That once a plan is worked out, you will be able to make good on your debts.

- That by working with you, the creditor will ultimately save time and money by avoiding collection or foreclosure.

- That you've been a long-standing customer, if you have been.

- Point out your sterling (hopefully) past payment record.

 The Key   You need to communicate openly and honestly with all your lenders when you think you may fall behind in your payments.

In this lesson, you've learned how to restructure debt with your creditors. In the next lesson, you will learn about getting professional help.

17

GETTING PROFESSIONAL HELP

In this lesson, you will find out where to get help if you can't handle it alone.

Financial problems can make even an otherwise accomplished professional feel frightened and alone. If the thought of putting the pieces back together by yourself is more than you can handle, you should turn to someone else for help.

FINDING HELP

Many groups and organizations offer debt counseling. Among these sources of help are the following:

- **Family Service Agencies.** These can be found throughout the country. They either provide financial counseling themselves or make referrals to local financial counselors.

- **Universities, Military Bases, and Local Courts.**

- **Banks and Credit Unions.** Most branches can arrange debt counseling for both customers and members.

- **Non-Profit Consumer Credit Counseling Services.** These agencies provide help to anyone that needs it.

Check References Make sure you're dealing with a counselor affiliated only with a non-profit consumer credit counseling service. Avoid individuals who claim to be credit advisers but do little, if anything, except take your money and disappear. Never sign on with a credit doctor or clinic that promises to clean up your credit report effortlessly. It can't be done and, more importantly, you won't learn how to avoid debt problems in the future.

To find assistance, check your local phone book under Human Services. Also, you can contact your city's Department of Social Services. Or, ask your local bank to recommend a reputal credit counselor.

Overspenders Anonymous An organization for people who have a chronic problem with overspending. Usually local chapters are listed in the white pages of your local telephone book.

CONSUMER CREDIT COUNSELING SERVICES (CCCS)

By far, the largest group of credit counselors is the network of CCCS agencies associated with the National Foundation for Consumer Credit.

Their mission is to help consumers understand how the credit system works and how consumers can better manage their money and credit. The agencies charge a small fee or collect payment directly from the creditors. If you use a consumer credit counseling service, it will be reflected on your credit record.

 CCCS To contact the National Foundation for Consumer Credit, Inc., write 8701 Georgia Avenue, Suite 507, Silver Spring MD 20910, or call 1-800-388-2227.

A counselor will first evaluate your situation and help you set up a payment plan. The repayment plan usually lasts from two to three years. You must agree to the following:

- To make payments to the credit counselor once a month, either by cashier's check or money order

- Not to incur any new debt until your repayment plan has been completed

Credit counselors give you moral support and concrete financial advice. They can:

- Help you set up a budget

- Negotiate with your creditors

- Walk you through your options

- Set up repayment plans

- Serve as a buffer between you and the creditors (some creditors view your involvement in a credit counseling program as a positive step because it demonstrates a good-faith effort on your behalf to solve your financial problems)

Finding a Financial Planner

Consulting a financial planner will cost more than seeing a credit counselor, but a financial planner can do more for you. A financial planner can help you with all aspects of your finances, not just with debt problems.

Title   Anyone can call themselves a financial planner, so you need to find one who's qualified. Seek out someone who has the credential CFP (Certified Financial Planner) or ChFC (Chartered Financial Consultant). Planners with these credentials have completed a rigorous training program, passed a comprehensive exam, and must have a minimum amount of experience as a planner.

The best way to find a planner is by word-of-mouth. Ask your friends, co-workers, and relatives. Ask your banker or attorney for a recommendation.

Unfortunately, erasing bad debt is harder than running up debt. It takes time and a lot of hard work. See Lesson 23 on how to rebuild your good credit standing.

In this lesson, you learned who to turn to for professional financial advice. In the next lesson, you will learn how to avoid credit problems in the future.

18

Avoiding Future Credit Problems

In this lesson, you will learn specific steps you should take to avoid credit problems in the future.

If you've had problems in the past, or are now working your way out of excessive debt, avoiding future credit headaches no doubt sounds appealing. You must consciously follow simple and smart strategies in order to stay on sound financial footing in the future.

Developing Better Habits

After you've established the habit of making regular payments to your creditors, use the same pattern for building your savings account. In fact, don't stop the payments even when you no longer owe someone else. Just continue making the checks out to yourself.

Deposit the checks into an emergency fund (see Lesson 6). This emergency fund is a pool of cash equal to at least three months of day-to-day living expenses. This is money that can be tapped quickly, without penalty.

When you have a cash reserve, you can stop worrying about how to make the car payments or whether an unexpected emergency will throw you into another debt crisis.

Having a cash reserve will:

- Give you freedom from worry
- Allow you to take advantage of cost saving sales to buy items that you really need
- Let you meet sudden expense
- Save you considerable sums of money in the long run
- Keep you out of trouble with debt in the future

CREDIT CARDS

When you do use credit, shop for the best deal. Look at each credit card offering, and then list and compare. Use the following table:

	CARD #1	CARD #2	CARD #3
Annual Fees	_____	_____	_____
Closing Costs	_____	_____	_____
Grace Period	_____	_____	_____
Annual Percentage Rate	_____	_____	_____
Penalty Fees	_____	_____	_____

Continue to monitor all credit spending practices. Charge only what you can afford to pay in full when the bill comes due.

To help find credit cards with no or low fees, contact Credit Card Holders of America, 560 Herndon Parkway, Suite 120, Herndon VA 22070, or call 703-481-1110. Or you can contact Bank Rate Monitor, North Palm Beach FL 33408, or call 407-627-7330.

CREDIT REPORT

Check your credit report annually (see Lesson 19). Make sure all the information is correct and complete. Be sure any accounts you've closed have been reported as closed to the credit bureau.

DEBTS

Keep your debt/income ratio under 20 percent. If possible, you should aim to keep it at 15 percent. If this ratio begins to creep back up, you should start cutting back your spending immediately.

BILLS

Get in the habit of paying all your bills on time. This enables you to avoid paying late fees and helps you to keep track of where you stand financially.

Bill Paying   Organize your bills by due date. Mark two envelopes with "due by 1st" and "due by 15th." As bills come in, place them in the appropriate envelope. Using this simple method should ensure that you don't miss any due dates.

SIMPLIFYING YOUR LIFE

The easier you can make the handling of your finances, the quicker you'll be able to find financial security. Always look for foolproof techniques to make your money management easier. Some of the methods available today are explained in the following sections.

AUTOMATIC BILL PAYMENTS

With automatic bill payments, the money to pay certain bills is automatically deducted from your bank account each month. You never have to worry about paying the bill on time. All you need to do is make certain that you have enough cash in your account to cover these monthly expenses.

 Account Balance   Be sure to allow for all payments deducted from your account balance to avoid an overdraft.

There are advantages to this arrangement:

* Your bills are paid on time.

* Automatic payments may qualify you for lower interest on loans because your bank's account management costs are reduced.

* Bill paying is simplified.

However, one significant drawback is having to keep enough money in your account on the payment date every month. If you forget and funds are not there, you will overdraw on your account and have to pay substantial fees, often as high as $20 per overdraft.

PAYING BY COMPUTER

Check into having some of your bills paid through your computer. Supply your online service (such as America Online or CompuServe) with the name of your bank and your account number. For each bill you want to pay, you'll need the following:

- The name of who the bill goes to

- The date the bill is due

- The amount of the payment

Allow four business days for the payment to be safely processed. You will pay about $6 a month to pay up to 20 bills.

The advantages and disadvantages are the same as direct deposit, except that online payment gives you more flexibilty in paying your bills because you can add monthly payments quickly as they come up.

DIRECT DEPOSITS

Funds are deposited directly to your account from routine checks you receive.

This may be the easiest way to ensure that you build up a cash reserve because you never handle the money on the way to your account.

Routine Checks   Checks you receive on a routine basis such as paychecks, social security, government assistance, alimony, etc.

The advantages of direct deposit include the following:

- You avoid long lines at the bank.
- No time is wasted between receiving the check and the deposit.
- You're safer not carrying around large amounts of cash.
- You may receive a free or reduced cost account with your bank.

IMPROVING PERSONAL FINANCE

Once you've mastered debt management, you should strive to improve your knowledge about other financial topics such as investing, risk management, taxes, and retirement planning. The more you know about personal finance, the better off you'll be.

To get this information, you can:

- Attend classes
- Read the personal finance section of newspapers and magazines

PUT AWAY YOUR ATM CARDS

Although ATMs are a wonderful convenience, they make it too easy for you to get money you really shouldn't touch.

HIRE A FINANCIAL PLANNER

Work with someone who can give you ongoing financial guidance in all areas of your finances. Try to find planners who will work with you to formulate a financial plan, rather than sell you products.

BALANCE YOUR CHECKBOOK

You need to know exactly how much you have in your checking account to avoid bouncing checks and paying high fees.

BALANCING YOUR ACCOUNT

Begin by collecting your most current checking account statement and compare all transactions listed against your checkbook register. Enter any transactions (deposits, interest, checks, withdrawals, ATM transactions) shown on your statement that aren't listed on your register. Use the following worksheet:

DATE OF DEPOSIT	AMOUNT	CHECK #	AMOUNT
_____	_____	_____	_____
_____	_____	_____	_____
_____	_____	_____	_____
_____	_____	_____	_____
_____	_____	_____	_____
_____	_____	_____	_____
_____	_____	_____	_____
_____	_____	_____	_____
_____	_____	_____	_____
_____	_____	_____	_____
TOTAL A	_____	**TOTAL B**	_____

Now compare the amount of each check, withdrawals, and deposits listed on your bank statement with the amount in your checkbook register. Then use the following worksheet:

Enter balance from most current statement	$_____
Plus Total A	$_____
Equals	$_____
Minus Total B	$_____
Equals your current balance	$_____

Help If the task still seems overwhelming, ask your bank or credit union branch manager for help. They're usually more than willing to help get you familiar with the formula.

In this lesson, you've learned some of the techniques that will help you develop good financial habits so you can avoid future credit problems. In the next lesson, you will learn how to protect yourself from fraud.

19

PROTECTING YOURSELF FROM FRAUD

In this lesson, you will learn how to shield yourself from credit card fraud.

With the ease and convenience of owning credit cards comes responsibility. You must assume responsibility for your cards.

PROTECTING YOUR CREDIT CARD FROM UNAUTHORIZED USE

To prevent someone from using your charge cards without your permission, you've got to keep track of who has access to your account numbers.

Open all credit card bills as soon as they come in the mail. Review the charges for accuracy. Check that all the charges are ones that you have made. Compare your receipts against your statements. If you find errors, follow the steps on correcting billing errors outlined later in this lesson.

Adhere to the following rules to limit access to your credit card information:

- Never give your credit card number over the phone unless you're the one placing the call.

- Keep the cards you don't carry in a safe place such as your fireproof safe at home.

- Destroy all carbon copies of your charge slips.

- If you charge your gasoline, don't leave your receipt in the machine.

- Never leave your credit card receipts lying around the house or on your desk at work.

- Don't lend your credit cards to someone else.

- Try not to place an order over the phone by credit card if there are people around who can overhear you.

- Don't throw out old statements without destroying them first.

- If you pay bills with your credit cards, make sure you can't read the account number through the envelope.

- Try not to use your cards within sight of someone you don't know.

- Never give out your account number over a cellular phone.

Handling Credit Card Theft

If your cards are ever lost or stolen, contact your credit card issuer immediately.

 Contact   To report a lost or stolen card, call the toll-free number listed on your credit card bill. Card companies usually have someone available to take your call 24 hours a day.

Always follow up your phone call with a written letter. This letter should contain the following:

- Your name and address
- The card or account number
- The date and time you found your card was missing
- The date and time you reported your card missing
- The name of the person who took the phone report

The federal Truth-In-Lending Act states you can't be held responsible for charges made on your charge cards after you've reported them lost or stolen. If you don't report the loss until after fraudulent charges occur, your liable loss is limited to $50.

Use the following worksheet to list all of your accounts in case you have to notify the card issuer:

CREDIT CARD	ACCOUNT NUMBER	TELEPHONE NUMBER
_____	_____	_____
_____	_____	_____
_____	_____	_____
_____	_____	_____
_____	_____	_____
_____	_____	_____
_____	_____	_____
_____	_____	_____
_____	_____	_____
_____	_____	_____

Additional List   As an added precaution, keep an additional list of your charge cards, account numbers, and card issuer's telephone numbers in your safe at home.

When your account is used without your permission, the maximum liability you face cannot exceed $50 per card. However, if several cards are stolen at once, your liability can swiftly add up. The quicker you notify the credit card issuers, the more likely you'll be able to limit your out-of-pocket expense.

Homeowner's Insurance   Check with your homeowner's and renter's insurance agent to make sure your policy covers reimbursement for any out-of-pocket expenses you may incur.

Of course, it's always better to avoid being victimized in the first place. Be alert and do the following:

- Always sign your cards as soon as you get them.

- Consider registering your cards through one of the credit card registration services. A single call to their main number will cancel all your credit cards.

- Don't carry all your cards everyday. If you're not planning to use one, leave it at home. This will limit your losses in case your wallet is stolen or lost.

- Always ask for your copies of credit card receipts. Save them until your monthly bill arrives and check the charge against the statement.

If, despite all your precautions, someone manages to obtain account information or your credit card number, immediately contact your creditor with the unathorized amount in dispute. You have to request that the charge be reversed and taken off your bill.

Act Quickly   Call and then write your credit card issuer within 60 days of receiving a bill that contains a billing error. Send a certified letter to establish proof of mailing. Keep copies of all letters in your files.

DISPUTING AND CORRECTING BILLING ERRORS

When you're certain that charges on your monthly statement are incorrect, mail a letter to the special address listed on your statement. Be sure to include the following:

- Your name

- Your address

- Your account number

Be sure to identify the error and explain why you're disputing the amount.

 Write It Out   The Federal Fair Credit Billing Act gives you certain rights in the event of a dispute, but only if you contact your creditors in writing, not by phone.

Collect back-up information that can verify your claim of error. Sales slips and cancelled checks will help.

Once a creditor receives your letter, it is required to:

- Acknowledge receipt of your letter within 30 days

- Conduct a reasonable investigation within 90 days

During the 90-day investigation, the creditor must do one of two things:

- Send you an explanation stating why the billing error doesn't exist or why you still owe part of the disputed amount. You must also be furnished with copies of any documents the creditor used to make its determination.

- Make corrections to your account (with finance charges on the incorrect amount credited to you). You must be sent a letter explaining the corrections that will be made to your account.

While the account is being reviewed, you don't have to pay the disputed amount. But, you are still responsible for the rest of the bill.

 Credit Limit The amount you dispute is still counted toward the credit limit you're allowed by some credit card companies.

In this lesson, you have learned how to protect your credit cards from fraud and theft. In the next lesson, you will learn how to read your credit report.

20

DECIPHERING YOUR CREDIT REPORT

In this lesson, you will learn the basics of reading and understanding your credit report.

WHAT YOUR CREDIT REPORT MEANS TO YOU

Having a stable credit history provides you with a vital base for all financial management. If your credit report shows problems, you may not be able to purchase a home, buy a car, or borrow money for any reason.

Credit bureaus provide the information that is used to compile your credit history. The bureaus simply act as clearinghouses, collecting records on your debts, bills, and paying habits. This information comes from your creditors, banks, and other sources.

Credit bureau records include files on addresses, marital history, occupation, employer, salary, and moving dates. This data is used by credit issuers to determine whether or not to accept your loan application.

Credit Report   A report that records the history of your credit information. It provides data to creditors who then rate your credit applications based on your past actions.

Each credit account report lists the following:

- The creditor
- The type of account
- Your credit limit
- The number of bank cards and charge accounts you have
- The terms of these accounts
- Whether you've had any special problems with your account
- Any court actions such as judgments, liens, foreclosures, or bankruptcies
- The amount of original debt
- Any outstanding balances
- A payment profile for the last 12 months, which shows whether you've made payments on time

Report Check   Review your credit report periodically to ensure that the information is accurate and up-to-date.

Obtaining Your Credit Report

Whether or not you're having trouble managing your debts, you should review your credit history regularly. Even a quick check can uncover information that's either incomplete or inaccurate. The sooner you correct your record, the sooner you can improve your creditworthiness.

 Creditworthiness   Whether you are considered financially stable and worthy of borrowing money from someone else.

There are three companies that handle the credit reporting business—TRW, Equifax, and TransUnion. (The addresses and phone numbers of these companies are provided in Lesson 11.)

To obtain a copy of your report, fill in a request form listing your name, social security number, address (both current and previous), and birthdate.

To receive a copy of your report, you will have to pay a fee that ranges from $2 to $15.

 Turned Down   If you've been turned down for credit in the past 30 days, you're entitled to a copy of your credit report by the credit-reporting agency that provided information to any prospective creditor at no charge.

Reading Your Report

Once you obtain a copy of your report, you need to know how to decipher the jargon used by the credit bureaus. At first glance, the words seem designed to be analyzed by computers, not by people.

Trained Personnel Credit-reporting agencies are required to provide trained employees to help explain the information found in their reports. If you can't read your report, call the agency and ask for help.

Each report consists of five parts. The first part is the identification part, which lists your name, birthdate, Social Security number, address, and employment history.

Next comes the credit history. This section lists the name and identification number of creditors who currently or previously had a credit connection with you, your payment patterns along with the date you opened the account, your credit limit, and the terms of your agreement.

The next section lists credit inquiries, or when any creditor requests a credit report on you.

The fourth section shows public records. This will show whether you've ever been sued and your case listed in public records.

The final part of your report is the section known as the consumer statement. You are allowed to submit a letter of no more than 100 words stating your explanation for any credit dispute.

When reviewing your report, use the following checklist:

_____   Is the personal information accurate?

_____   Is your correct employment information listed?

_____   Are all the accounts shown actually your own?

_____   Are any of your accounts duplicated?

_____   Are the court and public records all correct?

_____   Have the past-due accounts been listed accurately?

_____   Are the dates of last activity (DLA) correct?

_____   Are the account status reports correct?

 Account Status Reports This information shows your payment history for each account. This is crucial data that is used to determine whether you should be granted or denied credit.

In this lesson, you have learned some of the fundamentals of reading and understanding your credit report. In the next lesson, you will learn about your rights under the Fair Credit Reporting Act.

PROTECTING YOUR CREDIT RATING

In this lesson, you will learn your rights under the federal Fair Credit Reporting Act (FCRA) and learn how to protect your credit rating.

Unfortunately, the credit reporting system isn't perfect. Information can be entered incorrectly or placed in the wrong file. It's your responsiblity to make sure that your credit record is accurate.

The federal Fair Credit Reporting Act guards your privacy in areas involving your credit obligations. Under this law, you're allowed to challenge and correct the accuracy of any credit report information.

You are also allowed to obtain the following information:

- The names of everyone that has received copies of your report for the last six months

- The nature and substance of all information (excluding medical) that an agency has about you in their files

- The sources of the above information

- The names and addresses of the reporting agency that is responsible for your application being turned down

- To have all incorrect information investigated

- To have the credit bureau alert all agencies of a mistake

- To include your side of any dispute in the credit report

CORRECTING MISTAKES ON YOUR REPORT

Mistakes on your credit report can cause you heartache and financial distress. Mistakes need to be corrected quickly before your credit rating jeopardizes your financial stability.

Once you've obtained and reviewed your report (see Lesson 20), make a note of any errors you find. Send a copy of the report back to the credit bureau with clearly marked corrections.

If the mistake was made by the bureau itself, it's up to the credit bureau to verify the disputed information. If it can't confirm the mistake, the information has to be removed from your file. The verification process must be made within a reasonable period of time, usually about one month.

WHAT TO DO IF YOU'RE TURNED DOWN FOR CREDIT

If you're turned down when applying for credit, always contact the credit bureau and ask the reason for the rejection. There could be a legitimate reason for your rejection, or there may have been a simple mistake which can be easily corrected.

Under the Fair Credit Reporting Act, if the reason you've been rejected for a loan is because of information in your credit report, you have certain rights, such as the following:

- The right to obtain from the lender who rejected your application the name, address, and phone number of the credit bureau that was used

- The right to contact the credit bureau and receive a free report containing the information given to the potential creditor

Save and Copy   If you are turned down, you will probably be asked to send the credit bureau a copy of the rejection letter in order to obtain your free copy of the credit report.

- If you believe the details on the report are incorrect, you have the right to tell your side of the story (see the sample letters at the end of this lesson)

- The credit bureau must investigate the information you challenge within a reasonable period of time— no longer than one month

- If the burerau's information is found to be wrong, the bureau must amend the report (see a sample letter at the end of this lesson)

There's another law set up to protect your rights. It's called the Equal Credit Opportunity Act. Under this federal law, creditors are prohibited from discriminating by granting credit on the basis of the following:

- Race

- Religion

- Age
- Sex
- Marital status

Discrimination If you are convinced that your credit history justifies the amount of credit you are seeking and that your rejection was based on discrimination, contact the credit bureau. Arrange a conversation with a manager or executive. Tell them you believe that your request may have been treated unfairly and you want the matter reviewed as soon as possible.

TAKING ADVANTAGE OF SAFETY MEASURES

There are other rules that protect you when you're applying for credit. Try never to give in to pressure to borrow money when you're making a purchase; but if you do, be aware of the following safety hints that can help you after the fact.

COOLING OFF PERIOD

Whenever a credit agreement requires you to put up your home as collateral, most states grant you three days to review the agreement before it becomes binding. This is called "the cooling off period." If, at anytime during those three days, you change your mind, you're allowed to cancel the transaction.

Act Quickly   If the three-day cooling off period passes before you contact the creditor to cancel, you're obligated to stick to the contract.

High Pressure   The same law helps with high pressure in home sales. The three-day cooling off period also applies to agreements made with door-to-door salesmen.

The seller is required to give you two copies of a dated form that explains your rights. If you change your mind and want to cancel the contract, you keep one copy of the form and mail one back to the seller. That form is called the "right of recision" form.

Right of Recision   Allows you to cancel the transaction if you notify the seller within the defined time allowed. The notice must be in writing.

If the seller fails to give you a right of recision form, you may have even longer than three days to cancel. However, in these instances, it's up to you to prove you were never given the form in the first place.

Certified Mail   If you decide you want to cancel the contract, always mail the form back using certified or registered mail. Be sure to keep the mail receipt.

SIGNING THE NOTE

Usually, it's not in your best interest for both you and your spouse to sign the note for loans or any credit agreements. In the event you are unable to pay back the loan, creditors can only attach assets and earnings of the person who signed the note.

Be cautious! No matter what the lender may lead you to believe, if a loan is not secured by jointly held property, it doesn't legally require the signature of anyone other than the person requesting the loan.

SIGNING A BLANK FORM

Never sign a blank agreement, contract, or any other document if all the terms and conditions are not completely filled out. If there are any blanks in the document, draw a line through them if they don't require any information.

Verbal promises don't count! Insist that every detail be put down in writing before you sign, no matter how inconvenient it may be at the time.

 Read   Always read the document completely before you sign it. If there's something that's unclear to you, ask for a complete explanation.

In this lesson, you have learned how to protect your credit rating. In the next lesson, you will learn about bankruptcy.

22

MAKING SENSE OF BANKRUPTCY

In this lesson, you learn about bankruptcy, and how it affects your credit history.

Your worst financial nightmare may be having to declare bankruptcy. Bankruptcy means starting over, losing your possessions, and, of course, embarrassment.

However, bankruptcy is simply a tool and, like any tool, it can be harmful when not used correctly, but helpful in certain situations. The purpose of this lesson is to give you the information necessary for you to decide whether bankruptcy is a viable option.

Seek Advice   If you're considering bankruptcy, you should consult a professional for help. Talk to a well-trained credit counselor or an attorney who specializes in bankruptcy before you make your final decision. (Read Lesson 17 on getting professional help.)

Understanding Bankruptcy

Of course, no one should take bankruptcy lightly. This book is filled with alternatives you should consider well before this step is taken.

But when there is no choice left, bankruptcy can help solve many of your debt problems, and will put a stop to the legal actions lenders may be taking against you.

 Bankruptcy A legal proceeding that temporarily freezes your obligation for repaying certain debts while you and a trustee work out a plan for repaying as many of your credit obligations as you can.

When you declare bankruptcy, your liability for some debts may be completely forgiven or you will be allowed to repay less than your full obligation.

After you have worked out a plan, you repay your debtors from the sale of your possessions or from your income, depending on which form of bankruptcy you have taken.

Considering the Choices

Filing for personal bankruptcy usually takes one of two forms—either Chapter 7 or Chapter 13. Each one has distinct advantages and disadvantages. You must do your homework before you make an irreversible decision that will stay with you for seven to ten years—that's how long bankruptcy filings remain on your credit report.

CHAPTER 7 BANKRUPTCY

Also called "straight bankruptcy," this type of filing requires you to give up most of your property to a trustee appointed by the court. The property you surrender will then be sold and the proceeds from the sale paid to your creditors.

 Forbidden Chapter 7 bankruptcy forbids you from filing more than once every six years.

Certain items are exempt from liquidation. Your limits on what and how much is exempt will depend on whether you file under state or federal law. But, at the very least, you will be given a $7,500 exemption, which you can apply toward the following:

- Land
- Your home
- Other real estate
- A vehicle
- Your burial plot
- Business inventory
- Other personal property

In addition, your debtors may also exempt the following:

- Life insurance with a cash value of up to $4,000
- Up to $1,200 value of a vehicle
- $4,000 of household goods (up to $200 per debtor, per item)

- $500 of jewelry

- $750 of tools of your trade or professional books

- up to $400 of any property (called "wild card" exemptions)

You will also be able to maintain any payments from Social Security, unemployment, disability income, welfare, retirement benefits, and various types of illness and injury payments up to a set limit.

If it's important to you to keep property not usually exempt from bankruptcy, you should use one of the following three strategies:

- Buy it back. Get the money and pay for the item scheduled to be liquidated.

- Trade it for exempt property. You may be allowed to trade the total value of the non-exempt item for an exempt asset of the same value.

- Make an arrangement. Talk to your creditor about a settlement to pay off your debt without selling the underlying property.

For example, suppose you owe money on a car that would normally not be exempt in bankruptcy, but without the car, you can't work and pay off your debt. Your creditor may exempt the vehicle in order to allow you to earn money. This arrangement is called "reaffirming the debt."

Exempt Assets   There are many rules and limitations that apply to exempt assets. See your bankruptcy counselor for a more in-depth explanation.

On the other hand, there are some debts that won't be discharged by filing Chapter 7 bankruptcy, such as the following:

- Credit card charges made within 40 days of filing

- Certain back taxes

- Alimony

- Child support

- Personal loans and installment purchases made within 40 days of filing

- Many student loans

- Debts resulting from fraud or false financial statements

- Automobile accident claims as the result of reckless or drunk driving

- Traffic tickets or fines from breaking the law in criminal cases

- Money you owe to someone from intentional harm done to them

- Any of your possessions converted to exempt assets within 90 days of filing

CHAPTER 13 BANKRUPTCY

This is basically a reorganization of your finances. You are not required to sell off your assets in order to repay your creditors.

Filing Chapter 13 is only allowed for people who have a fairly stable income. You will have to present a repayment plan for approval to the bankruptcy court. If the court approves the plan, you will pay your debt through a court-appointed trustee.

There are advantages to using this type of bankruptcy filing:

- You are making a good faith effort to repay your debts. You can always point out to your future creditors that you made good on these debts, instead of having them liquidated under a Chapter 7 filing.

- You don't have to give up your possessions.

- It carries less stigma than bankruptcy under Chapter 7.

- It allows you to keep enough current income to meet your living expenses while you're working on paying off the debt.

- Some of the debt that isn't forgiven under Chapter 7 (tax obligation and student loans) are forgiven if you can prove they would cause you an excessive financial burden.

- You can file an unlimited number of times.

On the downside:

- You have to stay on a strict budget.

- Most of your earnings must be devoted to paying off your debt.

- The court can deny filing if they believe you are abusing the bankruptcy system.

- You can only file if your debt is within certain limits and you have a steady job.

Change of Status If you find your repayment schedule is not manageable, you can change your bankruptcy status from Chapter 13 to Chapter 7 at any time.

Deciding which form of bankruptcy to file depends on your circumstances. While Chapter 7 rids you of your debt obligations, it also rids you of most of your possessions. On the other hand, Chapter 13 allows you to keep your belongings, but your income for the next three years will be used to repay your debts.

When It Doesn't Make Sense

Bankruptcy complicates your life and makes it extremely hard for you to move ahead financially. Use the following guidelines to help you determine whether bankruptcy is your best option.

Don't consider bankruptcy if:

- Your bankruptcy could be challenged. Your filing may be challenged if there is evidence you have committed fraud or abused the system. Creditors use the following signs as red flags of abuse:

    - You've run up large bills on your credit cards just before filing for bankruptcy.

    - Your spending patterns have changed drastically lately.

    - You've taken out cash advances right before filing.

    - They suspect you've tried to hide property from the court.

- You've recently transferred assets to members of your family or friends.

- You've been incorrectly filling out credit applications with overstated income and understated debts.

- You have rendered yourself "judgement-proof." In the financial industry, this means you are a consumer who has little money and little property and no joint debts. If you were sued, your creditors would have very little chance of collecting their debt.

- You want to keep up your ability to borrow money. Even if you pay back your debt under Chapter 13, you may find yourself turned down for credit. Bankruptcy stays on your credit history for ten long years.

- You will lose possessions you want to keep. If you file under Chapter 7, any property not considered exempt may be lost to creditors.

- Your loans will be passed on to someone else. If you've had someone consign a loan, or if you have joint accounts, lenders can go after the joint applicant for repayment of your debt once your liability is discharged under Chapter 7.

BANKRUPTCY CHECKLIST

Go through the following items on this list before making your final decision:

- First, work with a credit counselor to see if there is a way to pay off your debts.

- Talk to a qualified bankruptcy attorney or credit counselor.

- Look at your debts to see whether they would qualify for discharge through bankruptcy filing.

- Read all you can about the two types of bankruptcy filing.

- Review your assets to see which ones you would use as part of your property exclusion.

- Make the commitment to see your agreement through to the end.

In this lesson, you learned about bankruptcy. In the next lesson, you will find out how to rebuild a strong credit rating.

23

REBUILDING
YOUR GOOD
CREDIT STANDING

In this lesson, you will learn how to rebuild your credit position.

If you've struggled through some tough financial times, and made it safely to the other side, it's time to reward yourself—not with a spending splurge, but with an improved credit outlook.

You should start with a five-step program. These steps will start you on your way to a better, stronger, and safer credit rating.

IMPROVING YOUR CREDIT RATING

Start by checking your credit report for accuracy. If you find mistakes, clear them up by sending a dispute to the credit bureau (see Lesson 21).

Bring all of your outstanding accounts up-to-date. If you have old accounts that remain outstanding, make them current. It looks better on your credit history to have all obligations paid up. Don't ignore the old bills that have already been turned over to a collection agency.

Avoid Court   Even old accounts can lead to a court date. Don't think creditors have short memories. Creditors have the right to take you to court, even if the unpaid bills are from years ago.

Put yourself in the place of your potential creditors. Creditors don't want to lend money to someone who doesn't bother to pay their bills. Furthermore, creditors certainly don't want to begin a relationship with someone whose wages are being garnished or someone who is having collateral repossessed.

Wage Garnishment   A way for creditors to legally obtain a percentage of your compensation in order to satisfy outstanding debt. A portion of what you owe is deducted from your paycheck before you're paid.

Update your credit record. If you have accounts that are current now, but used to be past due, make sure the past due statements are no longer on your credit record.

Write to your creditors and ask that old information be removed from your record. Write a polite and brief letter to the credit manager. Don't give in to the temptation to be nasty or threatening. It doesn't work.

Improve your references. If you have new creditors that have always been paid on time, make sure they let the credit bureau know about it. Try to set up a credit card account. (See the section on secured credit cards later in this lesson.)

Best References Credit cards can be one of the best sources of a positive credit reference.

Bargain your way to a better credit rating. Offer to pay off old past due accounts. Use this as a negotiation point with your creditors. You pay off the old bill and your record is cleaned up.

 Get it in Writing Be sure to get all agreements in writing. Don't take the chance that once you've made an agreement, you don't live up to the agreement.

By all means, when you've set the terms, stick with them. Once you've defaulted on your agreement, it's not likely you'll ever be given a second chance.

Obtaining a Secured Credit Card

If you don't think you can qualify for a standard credit card, try to get a secured card.

 Be Wary Unfortunately, there seems to be an overabundance of fraud when it comes to the secured card market. Shop for your card with extreme caution.

To determine whether the secured credit card you're considering is legitimate, make sure you find out what bank has issued it. If there is no mention of a bank, you don't want this card. Also, you should avoid any card that "guarantees acceptance." There is no such card.

Secured credit cards are backed by your own money deposited in an account at the bank issuing the card. Secured cards resemble other credit cards but they're for people who can't get regular credit cards.

 Check First Make sure the secured credit card you choose will report your payments to one of the three credit bureaus.

A secured credit card works as follows:

- You agree to make a deposit into your own account at the bank issuing the card. You must keep the money there as long as you hold the card.

- You then fill out an application for a secured card and the bank runs a credit check. The standards used are considerably more forgiving with secured cards than for a regular credit card.

- If the bank approves your application, you'll be issued a secured credit card, with a limit tied to the amount of the deposit in your account.

- You cannot withdraw your deposit until the account is closed.

- You use your card just as you would an unsecured credit card.

- When the bill comes in each month, you pay it on time.

- If you fail to make a required payment, the bank can collect its money from your account. Unfortunately, then, you lose the good credit history you're trying so hard to rebuild.

 Bankruptcy   If you've recently filed for bankruptcy, look for banks that will offer you a secured credit card. Some banks will issue these cards to customers even if they have filed for bankruptcy.

SIGNING UP WITH A CREDIT REPAIR COMPANY

These companies work with you to remove outdated credit information and contact your creditors on your behalf. If you don't feel up to handling things yourself, you may want to hire a credit repair company. However, be aware that these companies are sometimes disreputable and can leave you in far worse shape. Choose them carefully.

Use these guidelines when considering a credit repair clinic:

- Does the company have a license issued in your state?

- Is the company bonded?

 Bond   A type of insurance that helps guarantee you'll get your money back if the company turns out to be bogus.

- Does the Better Business Bureau (BBB) have any complaints on file against the credit repair company? If it's not registered with the BBB, forget it.

- What will the credit repair company do for you? How will your credit record be cleaned up? See whether you can obtain your funds if the clinic can't remove information from your file.

- What is the fee structure?

- Is there a cancellation period? If you change your mind before they begin working on your case, can you get your money back?

 Conflict of Interest   Has the service offered you credit cards or loans? Also, if the company won't say what bank it is affiliated with, you should assume the company is probably not legitimate.

Rebuilding a poor credit rating takes time and effort. Don't get frustrated by the slow progress. After all, getting in debt and losing good credit standing didn't happen overnight either.

In this lesson, you have learned what steps to take to get your credit rating back on track.

INDEX

T

temporary loans, 33-35
theft (credit cards), 101-103
     avoiding theft, 103
     disputing charges, 104-105
     homeowner's insurance,
        103
     renter's insurance, 103
     reporting stolen cards,
        101-102
     Truth-In-Lending Act, 101
true cost (mortgages), 36

U

unsecured debt (defined), 7

V

VA mortgages, 37

W

work-study grants, 39